Mortal Lullabies

¤

Ken Meisel

FUTURECYCLE PRESS
www.futurecycle.org

Cover photo by Margo Scott-Meisel; author photo by Anita Scott-Meisel; cover and interior book design by Diane Kistner; Chaparral Pro text and titling

Library of Congress Control Number: 2018939688

Published by FutureCycle Press
Athens, Georgia, USA

ISBN 978-1-942371-53-3

For Mother and Margo,
bookends in a living stream

Contents

"These mortal lullabies of pain
May bind a book, may line a box,
May serve to curl a maiden's locks;
Or when a thousand moons shall wane
A man upon a stall may find,
And, passing, turn the page that tells
A grief, then changed to something else,
Sung by a long forgotten mind."

—*Alfred Lord Tennyson, In Memoriam*

I

Song of the Dying as a Song

Like bittersweet nightshade
and grassland bitterroot;

like draperies, trailers, and
creepers of aromatic honeysuckle

wound in vine cleft and spiral,
down, along a sideways fence;

like the absent voice of a bird
singing the day into darkness

in the embrace of a shrub, you hear
the song of the dying as a song.

And once, in a lot of old Packards,
some of them so rusted

you could shove your hand
through them to find nothing there,

you heard the vibratory hissing
of insects, hidden deep underneath

the rusted chassis and down,
into the motor's vacated frame;

and inside the insects' stridulating
and scraping, you heard the song

of the dying as a song. And once,
alone, inside an emptied building—

while you were trespassing there—
you heard the groans of a hobo,

or a stray dog, or a phantom, or
the pleadings of an industry, long gone,

and when you heard it, you heard
it as the song of the dying as a song.

Invocation

Small god who wiggles silver light
across the garden fountain's

lofted wet edge,
who sprawls downward

like a crumbled maple tree leaf
at the side of the bench

just to hide yourself from
my watchful glance,

who ignites the cardinal flowers
with red,

why do you take the dead
to you?

Why, each season, are they
gathered back?

I take those who must die
because the color source

needs them—
just like the red of the geranium

and the blue-green
of the iris stalk

produce a flower of color—
so, too, does the world,

turning to its life again,
make over its hue.

December 9th, 1980

Red salvia, lime green chrysanthemum,
lonesome pots of geraniums, browning,

slowly decaying in the cold wind,
in the spotted, anemic sun,

the alcohol of autumn's mood
drowning the front lawn's color,

rose daphne shrubs, changing their hue,
the orchestration of birds in the trees

carefully awakening the oak tree's canopy,
the neighbor's bullied gutter,

and the soft, cracked egg of morning sun
spilling over the old, hard-edged porches,

over rows of parked cars, the soft-drink ale
of morning, fizzling over Hamtramck,

sad-like, lonesome, an effluvium of gloam
mixed in the morning's flirtatious glitter,

and the quick eruption of snow flurries—
winter white, a crystalline frizzante

surrounding me, taking me over—
stirring me into wakefulness again

as I step outside, smell the dawn,
take it deep into my nostrils.

The woman I left last night, already
a lost note of music, a transient feather

already taken by the evening's
calving of moonlight, by the night's

twilight cave, by a Sagittarius moon,
and John Lennon, murdered:

shot dead outside the Dakota Hotel
by a man composed of fear—

lost, erratic birds cloying at him,
tearing his mind from rim,

a pistol rising from his hand
like a pointed deformity—

and killing Lennon dead in a blunt
pitter-patter of gun-shot fire.

We listened to the news on the radio,
sat there sipping our coffee

at a kitchen table in Hamtramck,
my brother and I,

and felt the first bite of winter
coming on.

Vesper Sermon at the Cemetery's River

Oh you bellowing and tolling songs
of the anguished church steeples

lolling and lounging into the hard-acre
of the dusk's one assent to choir;

oh you howling police sirens,
you ambulances yelling onward

against the dirty gray patina
of the city's untidy horizon,

you bloated roar of bagpipes
moaning over rampart tombs

and the weeping angel statues
standing dismal in the gloaming;

oh you mordant croaking frogs
slopped at the river's wet edge;

you whispering, buzzing insects
with your tiny murmuring hymns

rising up, like a silent chanting,
through the damp slippery foliage

moistening these tombstones
where the cricket's choir abides;

oh you loose, bridal leaf gowns
of the matrimonial shrubs

bent to devotion and drinking
at the edge of this wandering river;

you sturdy brown belts of bark,
lying on the groom's name over

the hardpan crypts of dirt
where the moon's halo awakes;

oh you toad songs and private
sizzling dusk-born hymns and anthems

ascending over graves, over the lost
uncultivated foot-padding paths

where the priests and the mourners
stomp down the earth's sarcophagus,

where the ghosts of brides and
their grooms in floating halos abide;

oh you cries of the anguished
lovers in their grievous embraces

searching for their grace notes
to God, and to all forms eternal,

and for entry into that one final
carol and solar-creep home;

oh you quick peeps and chitters
of the burnt-colored nighthawk—

anonymous and solo and bright
as you dip and pull from a dive

with your mission of survival
as the gallant moonlight rises

over the wiggling gray water
moving, soft and easy, through

the veering valley train
of a cemetery's lost and its found—

oh do rise up into my heart
so that I might soar in you

in the way that the dawn—so aloof
and so indifferent, and so shrouded

in its courtesy of quietude
and wet light—ascends at once

so full of prayer: so awake and
so alert, with seeping sweet result.

Mortal Lullabies

Wood smoke and bramble weed,
dressing for mortal lullabies

and for this life's afterthoughts.
This for your living red cedar:

how the blood and bones scatter!
Small mandala of deer bones!

Once, a raccoon's striped tail,
lying supine on the trail's bend.

Once, on a mountain in Tennessee,
where you were captured by wind,

your tent, a hapless angel, lifted,
thrown down-slope into pine trees.

Once, in the ocean's wave swell,
where you saw your father's triumph

as he dove head-first into firmament
and lather. Once, with your brother,

when you watched him fall,
a cedar waxwing, to the soil.

And with your mother, alone:
when you saw her eyes open

like an oriole coming awake
after surgery, her life still vibrant.

Once, on a great waterleaf, you
saw a dragonfly land and sunbathe.

Once, alone, by yourself at last,
your thirst quenched, you cried

that long, silent cry that says, *yes,
I loved them all, these beings*

so precious, who have died.

Watching Bilal Fall

—for Bilal Berrini

Because in the Arabic, the name *Bilal*, or *Billy*,
    when spoken in its native
        Middle Eastern tongue,

means, "The Chosen One,"
    we watch Bilal fall.
        He *is* falling—

like a zodiac of chosen twilight
    from a dilapidated window
        high up in the Brewster Projects.

He has been rousted
    from his reverie—
        during his deep contemplation

of the city nudging her silver face
    through a wedding veil of clouds for him to kiss—
        by four who wish to rob him

right here, beneath the starlight as he skateboards
    across an abandoned basketball court
        bathed in late sunset,

and he's been shot in the face
    with a pistol and then laid out flat
        in a bed of weeds and debris,

even though he can barely
    speak English
        and even though the money

he's carrying in his wallet will later be spent
    on fast food and weed.
        And even as he is expiring,

he knows that all who vanish must at first
    rise up—
        like a flame climbing up

a twisted tree branch—
    and so he rises up
        to the highest tower

of these vacant Brewster Projects,
    to fall.
        And so we watch

his elongated, slender body
    spiraling downward,
        into woodpiles and bindweed.

He is aiming himself down, like a squid,
    into the ribboned twist and swirl
        of chaos.

Isn't this what the artist studies—
    the unpredictable twist
        and swirl of chaos?

Isn't this what we volunteer to marry—
    alchemists in artistry—
        even at the time of dying?

And so he falls like a squid
    freeing himself
        from the familiar

aurora of nerves and lather—
    from the lockup of his bone structure—
        like he is still within the instant,

even now, because the wonder
    of this experience
        is too aerial for him to miss.

And like all who have been chosen
    to resemble a star
        unveiling its five-pointedness

from birth robe to jawbone
    to white glissando matter,
        we watch him demonstrate

his falling—through the air like a supernova—
    into this cradle of plank wood,
        lying there like his coffin.

It's not the city's fault, you say—
        she was only the new bride in his eyes
                because he'd blessed her that way.

It's not the killers' fault, nor the Projects,
        for they were simply there
                to teach the meaning of how we are chosen.

And because he is the chosen one
        we watch him
                open his giant squid eyes

like a deep-water diver
        as he drives his gaze
                into the grid arteries of the savage city.

And he spins and he needles in—
        freeing himself of all matter—
                into his next graffiti splatter.

And from his mouth come the words,
        "I'm savagely wild. *I am*...."
                This is how I am chosen.

MD

He's against the idea of time,
deep down inside himself,
his stethoscope dangling
from his neck like a vestigial
appendage and his thermometer,
that tool meant to record
temperature extremes,
sticking secure in his pocket.
His hands are gloved in blue,
and his name tag, like a military
insignia, reveals his ER's label.
Maybe he took up this challenge
at age seven when he watched
his sibling die in a car accident,
this challenge to defy time
and reverse it, like a watch.
This seeming battle with death:
Time took on death's face mask,
the hours of suffering, like a war
that always ends in forfeit, loss.
This MD also wears a mask,
shielding his identity from death.
Maybe he's never recovered
from the tolling sounds
of a church's heartache—for
how long the bells of the steeple
rang at the edge of the funeral mass
when nobody else could comfort
the big sky above as it rained
and the leaves swelled with hail
and the streets flooded in brown.
Perhaps he's never fully recovered
from summer's yielding to fall
and the way that grass withers
and flowers discolor and yellow.
Maybe his occupation has
nothing to do with such lore
but, in fact, maybe this MD

is insubordinate by nature—
as a means of protest and dissent—
and he simply cannot abide
with the ways that death,
like a gray moving sponge,
marauds its victims into blind
trance and disarray by fogging over
their sense of time's hours
before it captures them, one
by one, into the sovereignty
of its somnambulant reign.

Sermon of the Mourning Dove

On the outstretched edge
        of the peach tree's limb
                you sing your mourning song

to the pearl-gray horizon
        becoming daisy white
                and mango orange

in the dawn's quiet lustre.
        All the other birds, loud, ecstatic,
                singing their daybreak songs

in the maple trees and the solid oaks,
        cannot hear you—they don't even try—
                as you lean your wide,

generous gray chest
        over the edge
                of this peach tree branch

and you mourn
        from your one
                red trillium heart

(—so full of its ripe loss
        and its burnt aching—)
                so that your disconcerted body,

capsized over
        on its conquered little gray stalk,
                can both give up

and exalt for a nest at the same time—
        which is the exact way
                that life

both expands and retreats in us,
        like an accordion,
                at the same time.

And you capture again
        and again for me
                what it is to be

a living being
>   with an emptying hourglass
>   set inside a rib cage

meant to protect us
>   —although it never truly does—
>   because we all

must find a nest in this life,
>   and then we must let it all go
>   —at the same time—

as we're hurled backward
>   and out-ways
>   by the long journey's

tempest and drain.
>   Mourning dove—
>   bird of the turning

back of stark feral night sky
>   into daybreak's lustrous sunlight
>   and the afternoon's

over-ripe radiance
>   fading into melancholic afterglow—
>   don't bring anyone

or anything
>   back to me right now;
>   instead, just let me

hold on and let go—
>   in the exact way
>   that you inhale and release,

from inside the red trillium
>   of your heart,
>   all that's disquieted

and emptied in you by your song:
>   sing for me—right now—
>   this mourning song

that says we're beings
>   made of soft laments
>   and nesting calls

on the twist and flare
    of the peach tree's
        extended outer branch

as the morning
    —so lovely
        and so indifferent—

comes rising up again,
    behind the blue horizon,
        to greet me.

Hear my prayers and missives to you,
    gray mourning dove,
        with your two ink eyes

hiding one of the encrypted
    chapters of the *Book of Love*
        inside them.

Solitary dove, with the streak
    of a clown's rouge
        smudged across your beak

like the blood of the recording angel
    carrying in it
        all the data

of our soul's nesting
    and all our subsequent
        bodily forgetting,

don't give anyone
    or anything back to me
        this morning.

Instead, just sing ahead of me
    this one
        melancholic exaltation

of how we nest
    in one body for a lifetime—
        and then we let go.

Ropes

I've seen them dangling,
these ropes,
drenched in kerosene
and engine oil
or piled like dead snakes
in a corner;
I've seen them dropping
down like skinny
legless lizards
from the dusty barn
rafters,
seen them trailing
alongside
a horse's leather saddle
as if jealous
or in love—
I've seen them curling
into mock nooses
and threatening
a grain boy
who empties the grain
here,
seen them smacked
by kittens,
ignored by pigs,
and webbed delicately
by the garden
spiders
or cut loose
by the angry cooking women
who manage here,
who sing the ancient songs:
ropes.

Aspects of Kelly's Death

When the boy stopped breathing,
it was because he'd lived one day
too long anyhow.

The parents gathered, and there was
only the noise of quiet machinery,
bleeping on, embarrassed.

It was sort of like a dream continuing on
after the dreamer had awakened
and he'd left the bed. Even the lights
of the machinery kept insisting it wasn't,
couldn't be over.

The heart breaks into a thousand
fragments of image and memory.
That's just the rule...

It's less important that the heart breaks
than it is *how* the heart breaks.
A broken heart falls out of pace
with the events that have broken it.
The stepping stones of grief catch us up.
And so the medical personnel, passing
the boy's dead body, were nervous,
and the parents, too, passed into a
kind of reluctance, and the boy,
up above them, watched, his two
eyes not really even interested.

*

Once, an hour earlier, there was
a nurse, a Filipino, who took the
boy's soft, extinguished hand in hers,
and she wept, and hummed a small
old island song to him about where
fishing boats go when they're lost
at sea. And who cares for them, then.

And then, an orderly pulled the sheet
over his head. It was a dry zip. *Crisp.*

The daylight, because it is curious and
explores everything, stretched a yellow
aura over the dead boy's dead body.

The bells of a church rang. I'm sorry
for that irrelevant little detail. I apologize.

*

The soul, leaving a body lying dead
on a bed, looks at first like a folded
blade of paper exiting a wound. And then
it puckers up, explodes out, and some
people think they see the northern lights.

The boy, lying there, was suddenly there
and not there. And he stretched, as if
he was exiting one of those clear plastic bags
that the dry cleaners put starched
shirts in, after they've been dry-cleaned.

In fact, the boy felt starched, *invigorated,*
really, before he was cleansed in light.

He escaped through the brick wall. He felt soft
feathers unfolding behind him. He flew free.

*

Here's an image of death I like, because it
settles the poem:

Then the last petal falls
from the rose onto the
white doily. And it sits
there, the petal, like an
anguished little boat,
something withered, or
stranded, dried out, like
a lone day of a week
gone beyond itself.

The mother sits there watching it.

The bells ring, and then there's
silence. The anguished hours.

Nothing is left but resignation,
and the dead solve that one
already for us. No need to ask.

What to do with the petal?

With the rest of a life that is gone?
When the years ahead lie awake?

The rest of the rose, well, that's
the body, and it's not relevant.

Mourning Song

By the red winterberry and the American holly,
the sumac's horn and the fat bladdernut,

by the meadow lark's drunk rapid bubbling
and the mocking bird's sneeze and its hiss,

we gather together, sing the mourning song.

By the low hum of an engine, at bank's edge,
where we fell flat to our knees to drop

the last remains of you in a mint julep river,
or still later, when we strolled in Ding Darling

to lay another's ashes in the tropical swoosh
of a stream's lacquer of liquor and mud,

or much earlier, when we froze silent in winter
and watched a casket pitter-patter down

into a mouth the size of a grave, and later
as we gathered in silence to open Christmas gifts,

we came, as one, to sing the mourning song.

It's always migration that we need to remember.
Always the dead—those bohemians—who

wander in our thoughts—even when we
fall, widespread and lost, in cities or in woods.

And so, to kiss goodbye on the wings a pearly
wood nymph, to listen attentive to the song

of a warbling vireo's rollicking leap notes
as it raises its milky white neck up to sing

in a hemlock tree, deep inside the woods
as one voice locks in grief with a partner's,

is to be at one: singing the mourning song.

II

Chopin's Prelude, Op. 28 No. 15

Troubled by the monotony of rain,
and fearful of your ill health,

you gathered yourself at your piano—
the rain scattering all around you,

pummeling the slick tiles and shrubs
of the Valldemossa charterhouse

and flooding the eager olive trees
and the rain-weary floral gardens

as it streaked the evening skies
with a jagged line of tarnish and dread—

and you felt, again, that lugubrious *hurt*
rise up in you—that lonely pitter-patter

rhythm of your heart's melancholy,
and that deeper fear that the world

at large could consume you, and
render all whom you loved, *dead*—

and so you dropped gently into a dream
where the rain steadily drowned you

while the storm outdoors—ceaseless—
colored the grounds pewter and jade

—the monastery's walls drenched in it—
and your fingers, asleep, *found it,*

this Prelude in D Major, this basso
ostinato that repeats the steady, dull

beating of the heart in all of us as we *wait*—
thick with the music of pulse, stop

and start—for grief, or joy, to come
make us over, console the hurt heart.

Uncle Joe's Song

—for Joseph Sunstum

High in your single-seat fighter, you rose and dove—

an aeronautics hawk as you breasted
the dark, ignoble sea, blotched and roving

with magnificent waves the color of chaos—

and you rose up again, trying to find
the very highest limit where the sky

could hold you safe, while you bulleted ammo
from the Royal Canadian Air Force gun ports

              of a *Spitfire* war plane

—down into the miasmic discoloration
of the land and the sea and the war—

and, when you thought you'd penetrated
the uppermost crystal of clouds where rain

became hail or became crowns of light,
a foreign object hit you hard in flight
and, swirling, you tumbled and fell—

into your country, your cemetery, your night.

The Song of the Letting It All Go

All morning, in the raspy vocals
        of birds
                chattering in trees,

and in the slow solemn march of deer
        grazing deep
                in the wood,

in the topsy-turvy argument
        of the stream
                rolling rapid over the stones,

you heard it in your ear, the one
        song of the letting it all go.

All afternoon, in the riptide
        of day-glow
                turning inward,

under the broadsides of plants
        turning amber
                and redolent,

under the maple tree turning radiant
        and colorful
                before emptying itself

all over the ground
        in a scattering
                of forlorn gold hearts,

you heard it in your ear,
        the one song of the letting it all go.

All evening, under the tolling
        of vesper bells
                in the church steeples,

under the high crest of clouds
        cloaking the new
                autumn moon,

under the vaporous streetlights
        casting shrill light
                all over the sidewalks

and down, over the river's
        green surrendering
                into aurora and light,

you heard it in your ear, the one song
        of the letting it all go.

Song for DS

—for Donald Ogilvie Scott

Sprawled out on the bed, your big hands
like oysters lying folded across your chest

like you were already inside your coffin
before your heart surgery even took,

you pulled me close to you, waving your
daughter off, and you told me to bring

to you *The Love Song of J. Alfred Prufrock,*
for I was to read it to you, before you slept.

And leaning in to you, reading the lines,
you closed your eyes, and you let the words

enter your quiet solace and your torment.
And when my tongue rowed over the sea's

marbled torrent—its waves lush with red
and green intensities, its landscape of shells

and other, misshapen junk of the deep and swell—
you let the poet's words amass in you,

and you lay your head back in reverie
and in a quietude meant only for dreaming.

And suddenly we were both at the ocean,
your eyelashes flooded with quartz light,

and the surrounding firmament of land
and ocean turned loud and disoriented.

And when you heard the poet speak
so easily of strolling in trousers on the beach,

you let your chest rise and wince and fall
as we trundled past the capsized skiff—

stormed and paralyzed there in the after-
squall of waves and froth and aqua-lather

where the sea gulls, like silly, after-supper
trolley keeps, lifted up and swooped

and then fell, dizzied, drunk, full of light,
their short, aggressive beaks tangled

with small crustaceans, popcorn, algae
and with the afternoon's fading coronets—

and when we stopped, you and I, to
ponder how the ocean blurred and softened

the sand, the shore, the entire strand
before the sunset and the sea-fall rendered

it agrarian, full of dark roots and pearls
and so many loop knots that we lost it

in the draw and deliverance of the tumbled
light that was expanding all around us,

you raised your hand above my voice to say:
the *mermaids singing, each to each,* are here—

to start their singing in the swirl and in the
waves and in the subtle falling shore light—

and when we spoke that line together, you
said: *I do not think that they will sing to me.*

And at the edge of the sea, where haze from
the horizon's hot exchange of immanence

and fervor spread, and the slip and fall of
sunset hit, mapped the rest of the aerial line,

one wave—advancing like a molten mermaid
with its hair on golden fire—rose at us, and

your daughter and I sat, our hands wrapped
around our legs, to watch it hit—and spread.

Whisper

What moved the leaves? What moves my heart, my legs?
—Virginia Woolf, *The Waves*

Listen: in the loosestrife, a perplexing voice;
in the nannyberry, and in the blackhaw's

heavenly bloom of white and ether flowers;
in the common elderberry's purplish balls

and in the viburnum's unpleasant odor—
a vagrant voice is calling to you; whispering.

Do you believe the body is on fire?
The sunlight, a halo, softening over the pond?

We who arrive here, wait it out, this day
when the column of light descends to us

and the rafters above us—so thick
with leaves and stars—collapse inside our dream.

When you knelt by me, *she said,* you felt
me enter your backside spine and you

stood up.
Now, you walk upright, with something else

inside you, some semblance of gushing
because you know that it—*this masquerade*

of pretending—is almost over in you.
Now, since you've heard the otherness of it,

this fireweed of change, surrounding us, calling
out to you—

from the pond's scrum and its weed zone.
And so it will be this way, from now on.

So it is: that the hard-stemmed bulrush of death
comes rising up from a vacancy of water:

so it is that we rise from an empty mirror—
so tall and so bold—and we attract a bird to us.

One bird, like a mocking cry or a screech.
Or a whistled huff or a one-note shriek.

Or a trio of notes, ascending, descending.
Taut with grief and sorrow, with sublime relief.

And so it is—*from this day onward*—you
must bend and listen

to that whispering bird over there—
that subversive, ceaseless voice that's forever

calling from the glass mirror of the pond's
overt reflection.

This is the window—where the whispering
mirror is. *This, she said to me...*

And she said: *sing the whispering song to yourself...*
Sing it until the sunset reddens the joe-pye weed.

Sing it—until you feel the loosening of the molecular
within you, and your tendons fill with light.

The bird is in the empty mirror. A trio gathers there.
The many faces are also there, waiting.

You must slow down. You must listen—
to that one-after-another trill and warbling:

to that one nomadic song of cellular unpacking
that's whispering beyond your leap.

So vagrant. So other worldly. So alone—
from your final undoing, from that unseen

dénouement zone.

Monk Crow's Song

Fevered in this life with a brain
capable of tumultuous rain showers

and electrical seismic mania,
you would stumble over

the sidewalks to your car
and lean across it like you were

shadowing it with your soul—
so as to gather to you

the car's vehicle number,
that number being its identifier.

The police would stop you
regularly,

just because you appeared drunk
while tearing the back seat

of the car apart in order
to locate a Kinko's receipt.

And when the police would
spread you out

across the vehicle to cross-check
you for suspicion,

you would refer them back
to the vehicle number

and tell them they should
verify your existence by

that number. Sometimes,
sprawled under a maple tree

and paging through a *Playboy*,
you'd be urged to move on

by an old woman, complaining,
and the police would arrive,

and, you'd inform them you'd
served your country in Vietnam

and had been exposed to
Agent Orange, and as they

commanded your license,
the proofs of your name

and your existence, you'd quote
Wittgenstein by telling them

that language "has a halo
around it," and thus we can

never truly assume to know
the true identity of the inscrutable.

And as they would pull you
away from the tree, you'd

ask them if they were familiar
with Nietzsche, who had said,

"to imagine a language means
to imagine a form of life."

Your life, when you passed
over, rebounded into me,

and, when I feel you, lurking
there, where you'd sprawl

in my room, I recall again
how you once told me that I was

acceptable to you because I
didn't try to understand your

inscrutable language but, rather,
just the manic glee in your face.

Car Accident

9th Street, St. Petersburg, Florida

The same month that woman
went into outer space—
and I mean Judith Resnik, who died
in the Challenger a few years
later, underneath the watching eyes
of God or NASA—
another woman I didn't really know either,
a common woman,
crashed herself into a telephone pole
in North St. Petersburg
because she was drunk and speeding
and she'd had one too many at the bar.
And maybe because whatever it is
that electrifies self-destructiveness
in the brain spit-fired disaster in her, too.
And so she wanted to *get it all out*
and smash it on for size
against something bigger....
Her family must've wondered why.
Perhaps she wanted to escape
from the night with the coolness of closed-up
shopping malls and the lonesome
ramshackle beach bum motels
and the lovers ghosting the windows.
Maybe she hated the smoky, paneled bars,
spotted alongside the beach roads
and their pulsing old juke boxes
playing songs of heartache
for the lonesome, clinging drunks
dancing against tomorrow.
Perhaps she drove against the small
banalities of her thoughts
or against the ledger of her failures
that kept knocking her back
into her final insignificance
and into the stubborn palm trees

planted to beautify a sad, aging
fisherman's city
stuck on the Gulf of Mexico
that, because it was sad,
kept on shining
anyway under the sun.
Maybe it was for the smell of fire smoke
clinging like invisible fingers to her jeans
that made her wish
for the salt of a man to grab her
in her bed at night, and comfort her,
and take away all her burdens.
And maybe, also, for the men
who'd wronged her, had stolen love
from her.
Whatever it was that made that woman
get angry, or lonesome,
or whatever it was that made
that other woman want to fly
up into the Universe, past the earth,
I can't really say...
but I do know that jewelry,
and men's love, and a baby
weren't reason enough to keep either
of them here....
We're all astronauts.
The heart owns its terrible burdens.
The heart breaks the strings
of pearls that are its ambitions.
You could hear the crash
and then, the silence.
And, then, there was the eye-popping
shock that followed,
the loud snap like a door,
where the brain tells the legs to run.
Whatever else happened then,
whether it was commotion
or the survival of her drunken soul
climbing out of the wreckage
like a torn piece of jellyfish

soaring way up high to the surface
and trying to figure out
if it had turned into a ghost
or an angel,
or some angry, electric sparkling
of her brain's gray matter
swimming up out of bone
and into the blanched humid night,
I can't really say.
All I remember is that the radiator
blew up.
And then there was that hissing
that tells you the smashed car,
because it's enraged,
is about to explode.
Sometimes, because we see it,
this light, this moon
shining above us like something
avenging something else,
like some engorged bird
seeking shelter in a tree,
we fill in the gaps,
the hands full of nothingness,
with whatever else there is.
I guess it's the way we tell ourselves
what to see and what not to see
and what to remember or to forget.
For me, I was watching
Johnny Carson with my father.
And my sister had given birth to a boy.
We'd just talked to her.
She was nursing him.
And putting him into his little bed.
And, outside, where the moon
slid behind a veil of moving clouds
and the crickets by the creek
had started up their chirruping
behind the apartment building,
I called an EMS
even though I knew she'd be
a goner—

because I couldn't think of anything
better to do
and because it was better than
doing nothing.
Then I hit the front hood of the car
with my one live fist
to stop it from that awful shrieking.

Poem for a Homeless Woman

—Rome, Italy

I don't know what to make of the condemned bag lady
   who's probably my wife's age—
      and who is lying in a soiled heap with her life's belongings

sprawled in chaos beside her, here on a side street in Rome,
   where just around the corner from me
      girls play hopscotch beneath a row of cypress trees

in a small city park while two young mothers sit drinking
   their evening coffee, and they go on chatting
      about their belief in God.

Maybe it is simply bad luck that her human dignity is wasted—
   and that her skin is diseased
      with the red decretals of poverty and ugly scratches

as the chiming vesper bells of Santa Maria Maggiore
   ring for another round of Mass.
      Maybe life's master plan for her is more about the study

of a lost soul shifting inside of a motherless body—
   or the way that the body actually forms around an expulsion
      from Eden, or around some kind of a prayer for salvation,

or when it's met with earthly ruin and for someone to witness it.
   Mercy is the grief-work of God,
      you whisper gently to yourself—

trying to comprehend futility. And futility is when life
   blinks an eye to let time absorb something.
      I hope her deliverance comes soon.

The police come by and they scoop her up and they roll her away
   like filthy dough. Drop her beneath a small park bench.
      I move over and I sit close enough to hear the thunder

of her voice praying to the open chapel between trees.
   Her hands reach up into vacancy. Into some absence of mother.
      I sit still, absorbing her into this poem.

The Small Sculpture Angel

—Mt. Kelly Cemetery

The small sculpture angel,
writhing over the resting
stone, her cement hands
clasping a bouquet of someone's
grieving funeral flowers,
seems at first to you
to be *alive*—her face, so
tender and flushed chaste
with afternoon sun, her eyes
occupied with insects and moss,
her small gown, dirtied
by the season's robust
and feminine floral platter,
and her tiny toes, emergent
like rose beetles as she
freezes here in perpetuity
as you move closer to her
to find her chronicle
and her sculptural falsity,
so immanent and so still.
And as you roam here,
where the graves are
solemn signatures of silence,
you discover that she
is not even alive here,
and she is *nothing*—
compared to the mother
and her young daughter,
these grievers you witness,
so *alive* still, and so *vast*,
with their own bird hands,
like raw crows, slashing
the roots and pottage out
where the graves—
those silent tableaus
of lost hours and echoes—
wait for living angels—
those reliquaries—to come.

Limelight

Lord, you shoot your paintball color
    straight up through the petals
        of this orange lily

sprouting through cracked pavement
    alongside the Temple Bar—
        in Detroit—where I sit

at a stool reading how the angry man
    shook his twenty-one-month-old baby
        back and forth

like he was doing some kind of polka dance
    with her—until the baby lost
        the light behind her

daffodil face—
    and she dropped vacant
        with the dull grace

of a pool hall ball. It makes no sense
    how the light explodes right through
        the lily face—

as if you, Lord, couldn't quite recall
    how to shove the straw
        of color into something

already alive and willing, a lily, oh Lord,
    and so you did so violently,
        abruptly—

as if all life is in vivid color,
    fermented in holy fire,
        some radiant limelight.

Even the shoeless woman
    fumbling with
        the brown bag of liquor—

gulping it like she's
    a vampire drinking
        the red blood inside your

carotid arteries, rambles on
    about the mania
        of the orange lilies

growing from the forgettable
    side grass along the wall
        of this bar,

even as she grabs hold of one,
    fingers it up to her mouth
        like it's a tootsie roll.

God, we become psychotic creatures
    when surrounded by
        innocence

and beauty—like we're attendees
    at some high school dance,
        impulses raging—

and we don't know what to do
    but yank at one another,
        stretch and pull

at one another,
    suck the temper of light
        from mouths

like strings of taffy.
    Even the jukebox can't take it,
        this song, *Love Hurts*.

Lord I remember her,
    my child, my fireball
        of radiance,

as she raced so fast
    across that park
        where her mother

and I were sitting together,
    trying to work back
        into our marriage

from some pull and tug
    of a polka dance we were doing
        with each other,

because we couldn't handle
   the taffy of romantic love,
      just couldn't.

And how that child raced up
   to greet us
      on a summer night

as the dusk marched in—
   draping the monkey bars
      in obsidian—

and how her face, like an orange lily,
   like a quick streak of light,
      brightened up

with limelight—
   glowed like a firefly
      as she grabbed

hold of our necks to embrace us.
   And my wife and I
      cried so hard

when she ran off to climb
   the monkey bars.
      And we had a chance

to watch her and cry some more
   at how the moonlight
      colored her orange

like a lovely lily as she played,
   while we made our way back in again
      to our romantic love.

We are swords of light, I fear,
   cutting one another
      to bits.

We are the limelight that aches—
   as it cozies up against the side
      of a wall—oh Lord of color.

Come back to me, sweet child
     who followed the moonlight,
          rolled over in it:

come back and dance your festive
     dance of fireflies
          beneath the lonely stars—

so that I can feel again the lullaby
     of your innocence:
          what you gave

to your mother and me
     as we watched you
          dance that night.

I long for it—this dance we do—
     this limelight
          that holds us tight.

Grief

Is a pinch on your index finger

that tears your heart
right through it,

like all your memories
are torn on a blue silken sheet

and pulled through the eye
of a top stitch needle,

and, even though you don't
want to feel it,

this tearing of yourself
open, this grief,

this cascade of hot anguish
brokered by mourning,

and by the eternal loss of someone
you've loved

and held deeply to your
chest,

and even one you've attached yourself to—
as if in an eternal embrace

so as to never
let go—

you are still moved by the rising familiar face
of someone kissing someone else

in an afternoon's startled
dream

because your heart asks for it,
this awful necessity,

this tearing of yourself open,
for love.

These Days

I get up early in the morning these days,
listen to the last persistence of crickets

rubbing the stars between their legs
underneath the bushes in the park.

Squat low to the window ledge and listen
to the laughing sound of my one child

playing on the swing in the park all those years
ago when she wore her hair long to her waist

and I brought a plate of peanut butter cookies
out to the monkey bars for all the girls to eat.

I hear the girls laughing until a bird in a tree
shrieks the first ribbon of morning here.

Press my ear against the screen to hear her
boarding the train, falling tired against the seat.

Open the book she is reading as she bites
the apple and sighs the last of her day out.

I imagine her feeling her heart-song until her eyes
close and she is slumped and dreaming a dream

that has a painting of a rainbow parading
over the gray buildings of San Francisco Bay—

as the morning fog rolls into the homes there—
and she blesses herself into her thirtieth year.

Watch her as she leaves the ceramics studio,
pottery in hand, to offer the world her gift.

Tip my ear for the nighthawk's final
feverish yelp as the evening's black clot

is slowly torn open into the gray morning—
and the roadside around me fills with cars.

III

Kevin's Song

—for John and Gail Urso

Kevin's asking me again what I think of suicide,
    grinning at me as he asks it,
        his bright eyes like moonstones,

his restless hands roaming over
    the top of his coffee cup,
        receiving the warmth.

"Imagine it," he says, "without the fear,
    without the sense of being tethered
        to an obligation to stay—

kind of like my dogs, unleashed, unhinged,
    freed to roam and wander—
        a thread, unstitched from hem."

I ask him why he thinks of such things
    at this time of his life, and he asks me,
        "Aren't we just musical instruments

in the end—violins, cellos, banjos—
    each wrestling with the technical
        difficulty of an étude?

Aren't we just études, compositions meant
    for the practicing of some kind of outcome,
        some perfectible leaving—?"

And he says, "I don't think I want to stay here,
    wrestling with this matter of my living—
        this is my end composition,

this seems to be my song, how it is I occur—
    no one seems to understand it,
        how it is I occur in this way."

These conversations are becoming
    a kind of theme for his struggle:
        his words, his quotations, his conflicts

communicated to me, like short, practiced
    musical scales; like quick cello swells;
        like roaming octaves and trills

and double-stops for the cello étude
    he's beginning
        to resemble;

his sloped shoulders and his tanned cheeks,
    browned by the heat-stroked, summer sun;
        his body, rounding

itself into the polished figure eight of a cello
    as he rubs the excitableness of these
        soft, quick-spoken words to me

into his tense, crinkled forehead,
    into the muscled pegs and purfling
        of his rib cage and his shoulders.

There's no argument I can say back to him,
    I think to myself as I hear him
        telling me he wants to leave.

There's only a nodding I can give to him;
    only a kind recognition of his occurrence
        filling me with wonder—

this étude melody of Kevin leaving the world—
    this idea of Kevin's suicide;
        this announcement of his choice to go.

"Isn't this what we actually do?" he asks,
    "This, being that we practice
        the one single idea of our

occurrence right on through to its
    technical difficulty, and then
        to its ultimate finish at the end?"

I tell him we *do* resemble luminous strobes of light,
    banjos and cellos of expansive
        streaming and vanishing;

it is true, we are the banjo and the broken box string:
    all this plucking and twanging of our uprising
        and falling into source.

Even the cello is said to be
    the instrument that carries the greatest
        likeness to the human voice, I say—

which he enjoys, and then he scoffs at me,
        tells me, "You're just poetic nonsense—"
            and then he says, "We're able

to split open—this is the one
        true end point of our dancing and our dismay:
            our human bodies

will crack open like shattered bodyboard
        of a cello splitting in two
            under the lustrous mid-afternoon sun,

and every musical note that we are
        will be released to roam free again,
            will rise up, like feathers, in air.

All of who we are
        dares to split open—
            into death, or into passion.

Something in us is so wild and untethered
        to anything that demands us to stay:
            some deep part of us

is so rabid and eager
        for an experience
            of, well, *leaving.*

And the hit parade
        of memories and namesakes
            inside us:

your love of me, mine of you,
        and all the pet names and gifts we give
            to one another—

from love, from open-heartedness,
        from fear and dread
            and from desperate admiration—

goes into these cells, into our body's deep core,
        and then they're all released, haphazard,
            into this indifferent wind

blowing through the green leaves
        on the rose bush here beside us—
            until yet another unruly musical

wind sweeps them all away from us here;
    and we're quieted down—our cells
      and our emotions—

and all that remains of us is broomed—
    like so many red petals and leaves—
      into the wind's soft drapery...

That's what I'd think death
    would *feel* like"—he says—
      "It would feel like

one petal after another
    lifting free of a red-rose bloom
      until there is nothing:

because we are just a strung necklace
    of created musical blooms, clinging
      tightly to a cello—

and when we are played
    enough in this life
      we do lift away, free."

And then he shifts steadily
    in his chair, and offers me this:
      "I think, in our clinging here,

that we become entangled out of habit—
    like rose bush branches in each other's
      starved spirits—

and we hold on,
    one nerve ending of our confused will
      to endure here

locks tightly to the whole deep center
    of ourselves and to the depth of another;
      and isn't that what *wanting* is—"

he says—"this insistent, thorny urge in us
    to cling, and to hold on to anything solid—
      no matter the injury

to self, inside the longing for another?
    And we agree that we must, somehow, you know,
      invite this, oh so ceaselessly:

this promise to one another:
    I will remain here for you:
        even though I'm weary—

from love, from want,
    from burden,
        from sorrow,

and from holding on so tightly
    to myself, and to the fullness of you—
        in order to prove

over and over again
    that we are fixed here, and devoted enough
        to remain here, to stay?

And isn't that love," he says,
    "this devotional composition
        we play—like a song—

into and out of each other's
    musical core? We are the being
        that frolics on the strings of love.

Wanting and devotion are the bargains
    we live by," he says,
        "they soften our aloneness...

And that's love, you know," he says,
    "this singular involvement
        that we gift to another—

this gift that fills up the cycles of our
    aloneness and our isolation
        with the fullness of an embrace;

and that's because we can't help but feel
    our homesickness
        inside each other,

we *are* each other's lifeboat of refuge—
    we do row ourselves
        into each other's hearts;

and, you know, in so doing, we
    claim one another;
        such is our drive to take port—

and that is no act of cowardice, to claim
　　and be claimed—
　　　　it is a courage to be claimed...

And the claiming of love roots us here:
　　and in so doing
　　　　it pays the wage for this fraction of time.

And so we should never be afraid
　　to love one another
　　　　with a brave, expansive heart," he says.

"But I tell you," he says again:
　　"it's all a pearl inside a magician's purse—
　　　　"it's all an illusion—

this fixed idea we're meant to be secure in a body
　　and convince one another
　　　　that the pearl remains in the purse.

Wanting is just the way that we fool
　　each other with kindness
　　　　that death will come much later.

Despair and loneliness (those states that terrorize us)
　　are the thorn birds of all our suffering:
　　　　and both are wearing my face;

both live inside the smile at my mouth,
　　and in the crinkled crow-light of my eyes
　　　　as I look deep into you:

And this empty canoe
　　sitting inside my rib cage is the rowboat
　　　　that will now take me, far, far away from you..."

And, leaning forward into my face,
　　he offers me
　　　　this single epitaph for himself:

"I tell you, the vibrant
　　pilot-flame burning inside
　　　　my rib cage

that is this living pearl, this soul in me,
　　will be fired up like a rootless yellow bird
　　　　into the orange shallot tea

of this setting sun,
     melting the sailboats, softening the bay.
         And I will mix

myself into the low,
     dusk-born charcoal breezes
         as they maraud

this sand-strewn beach;
     as children hold hands
         with mothers, ankling the waves.

And I will bloom into an exalted yellow canary flame
     rising above the satin-rippled waves
         smoked blue with sundown.

And my arrow-shaped little body will unravel
     into a careless wind-sweep
         of sloop notes and yellow feathers

blowing boundless across the desolate beach
     as sunset
         pearls into shades of coral

and butter, melting on the cheeks of the shore.
     I tell you this—" he says to me—
         "so that you will know

that we are beings inerasable but empty,
     we are indelible but free. We leave
         and we expand, elated, loved, indifferent,

and what is left of us is made of rhythm
     and echo: we're
         the tolling time bell that empties..."

He tells me this as his eyes light up
     in small, vaporous flames,
         and he adds another thought:

"Death is the inviting rowboat *beneath* all wanting,
     and it's the way the light rays,
         crossing the brain,

sing to us our final unrooting."
     And he sits there, watching me
         hearing him saying this, and he says—

"Perhaps your identity is caught there,
    too—
        inviting me so sweetly

to remain here, sipping my coffee with you:
    and you're vibrating on a taut cello string—
        you're one musical étude

practicing yourself
    for an unscored momentum of days
        as you mourn for me."

And he shifts easily now in his chair,
    sips on his coffee,
        adds these final words:

"I tell you, we are four strings—
    cut against fingerboard rosewood,
        and we're made of a cello's sweet sound

and also its wolf-tone counter-vibration.
    We exist—above a wildly fluctuating
        uncontrollable tone.

And it is this wild, fluctuating, uncontrollable
    wolf tone that sends us *expansive and discordant*—
        into our life and our perishing.

Perhaps you and I, together, are caught just now
    on the wolf tones
        of a string-to-body *counter-tone:*

and I am becoming two enflamed strings,
    ecstatic with my own canary light dissolving.
        And as my two strings swell with sound,

my canary light rockets against your body,
    still dense with this weight,
        and we do counter-resonate

into *wolf-tone-discordant vibration*—and that's just this *grief:*
    and only through a swift roll
        of the cello bow

vibrating against these four strings
    that now tremble
        with repeating cycles

of excitation and release—
        this one cello bow
                that we both hold

in our hands here together
        that *is* the magic wand
                that fixes a note here, or frees it—

will we be allowed to let go on the strings
        and be free to expand into vibrations
                separate from one another."

He tells me this as he stands up
        to leave,
                the lights of the room dim.

"We're one song
        of sheet music written
                to completion, we are."

And he says to me,
        eyes blazing like
                flames of excitable stars:

"We're beings composed of musical notes
        most beautiful, most expansive,
                most evaporative and free...

I think this is my song, it's mine,"
        he says to me—
                "Sing it

Mr. Poet who writes my words down
        on a piece of paper
                with his black ink pen

and his broken banjo heart
        made of its protest melodies
                and its wolf tones

barking inside all these counter-vibrations—
        sing it and play it until
                my name goes careening

off wood into salt spray
        and bounces over the capsized fishing boats
                being drowned by waves

until they resemble flipped cellos,
      rolling and keeling sideways
            in the drumbeat of the sea,

until all you can hear of me
      is the sharp echo inside your own brain
            where my song remains..."

(My dogs, chasing one another like smoke rings
      until light
            nudges them into ember and dark,

until the sunset, bold and stark,
      cuts them down into
            silhouette and shadow

and I follow them into the curtain of darkness
      sinking behind the sun's yellow lemon,
            away.)

"Sing this one occurrence
      of my song
            to those gathered

near to you one day;
      those who'll have the opened ears
            to hear."

IV

Song for the Parents Who Lose Children

Like a quiet group of concerned citizens
standing around one another in a lonesome port—

awaiting the guaranteed flow of new arrivals
to sprawl down a wooden plank from a docked ship

as they arrive—the parents who lose their children
to death convene. You can see them as they wait,

politely, for their lucky number to fall in.
And, like a solemn group of Heaven's carolers

preparing to lift their exposed throats up to sing,
you can wait for the parents who have lost their

children to death to mouth the names of
the lost as they sing. And once, watching one

of them mouth the child's name, I saw in her eyes
the blond light of the child's hair and the spring

blue in his little periwinkle eyes, and I learned
that the parents that lose children see them in color

as they sing. And for the parents who lose children
to eternity, you can always know that at night

they walk gently to the child's room just to hear
the long clear note, followed by the stuttered warble

of the lost child, finding a way in. And, for those
who lose children, those who roam the staircases

at night, one can always know they will smell
the child's downy, serviceberry skin, as both arrive

at the top of the stairs; and, so, one must always
prepare for that scented aroma of vapor and skin.

And for those parents whose children death takes,
there is always the tangle of dreams that arrive

at night: those lathered dreams where the child,
small or grown, floats back like a thrush on the wind—

right into waiting arms, and they sing. And in these
dreams, the parents, like an audience gathered,

remain stilled there, right inside the dream's haze,
and something of them never leaves it, this dream—

this holding on to their child as the child warbles
and sings and flutters up and down on brief wings—

because to leave it would be like turning their eyes
away from the child-bird flying hapless over a steep

cliff before soaring off it—and so the parents
can never leave it, this clinging to the dream. And some

of the parents, deep in the dream, do lift their fingers
up to touch the cheeks of the child before they

both step backwards—parent and child—to part ways.
And for these parents—those that do leave the dream

and let the child fall away from the cliff into the air—
the children who love them depart, and arrive back

to their first tree, and, like thrushes, they encircle
a fire—some concentric circle of consistency created

from a flame, and a line of flight marks radiating out
like a white halo—and they mimic every melody

they've heard while alive here, so that when they
return to their bodies, they recall every name sung

to them by the parents who've claimed them to life
here; and, deep inside them, the children, reborn

again, carry within them all the faces of the parents
who have given them birth here, time into time, again.

Dwayne's Song (Child of the Moon)

Sweet child of the moon, I see you
standing there alone on your front lawn,

your chocolate popsicle in hand,
your eyes drooling up at me.

Your mother, alone on her couch,
the needle in her arm, and your father,

alone in his cell, another tattoo
on his arm, your picture on his wall.

Do you see the radiant stars?
The fireflies so delicate, lighting up

the sunken shrubs? Do you see
where the face across the moon

is your sister, rising up for you,
and the stars, your brothers,

so many of them you cannot count?
Somewhere, beyond you,

where the fires burn at dusk,
and the clouds dissolve in indigo,

and the windowless buildings
of the city gather their olive glow,

you will find the crow flying
noisily alone there, past you,

and you will follow him, past
your mother and your father, past

the bridge stretching over the water
where the moonlight is ochre

and the angel's trumpets, strangled
into the trees, shout out your name.

And, when you hear it, your name,
your heart will fill with it, your name,

and your blood will carry awe,
the first kiss of desire, and you will

become the mystery to yourself, oh
angel of representation, oh lonesome

wolf-child who carries the heart
of a deer inside the arms of a bear.

And you will be one of them who
gathers varied shelters and departs;

who leaves the angry drill tone of those
who mangle the face, injure the heart;

who loves because the eternal rests
inside you, so vacant and emptied;

your ribs, a balustrade of bone rails
and a sash window, holding you in,

and your small face a radiant moon-
stone, your eyes, singing, igniting.

And then you will leave them, these
broken starlings that are your parents,

this town so desolate and alone,
so baked in clamshells and pollution,

and you will rise up, full of music,
your heart, spilled open, full of stars.

The Wind's Sermon (at the Cemetery's Pond)

Joe-pye weed, and feisty dame's rocket,
plants whose color outlasts the dusk.

And yellow iris, rising like a taut sword
from the pond's unsettled water linen—

like some triumphant afterthought
to the storm's recent, forceful passing.

In the reduced pigment of the storm's
surface color, the gravestones emerge

as solid pillars, markers for the day's
iron-colored preservative and glow.

And these ducks—mallards, gadwalls—
roamers on any surface's discontent

strobe left to right, right to left, in search
of the undercurrent's private wealth

of offerings. They seem to settle me
and calm me, soften my heart's *unevenness*.

Aren't all our movements into solace?
Left, moving into right, and right back into left?

Our eyes—roamers—like these ducks,
in a constant hunt for something sweeter?

Perspective, being nature's endurance
upon the fixity of every other shaping—

and this motion, this waving otherness
of the air, like a paintbrush, sweeping

every other fixed and existent color object
(*yellow iris, spike rush, great blue skimmer*)

against the rhythmic, streaking dynamo
of an audacious chance and change?

How it is the injured body *disorganizes*,
empties out, *is emptied,* by audacious wind—

by an emotional death, by a loss intensity
too overwhelming for the body's shape:

and then, thereafter, becomes a wave
and *quick vibration,* a sudden dynamo, and

a migratory leaping into another threshold.
Isn't that—this timeless leaping into *furor*

(that old word for enthusiasm, or mania,
which always transfigures what delays it)—

what all this mourning forces *awake* in us?
That furor—of immanence and eruption

into *newness*—that grief insists we seek?
The dismantling of a loss by *sumptuous wind.*

All these particle cells we thought we were
subjected to reorganization and change.

I'd like to believe that this is truly so.
All the deeper faith in my body *believes.*

Statue

Statue of a weeping angel, wings opened wide,
feet planted in a stance of sudden landing,

and immortalized here on this cold stone monument,
your mouth frozen in an astonished O,

as if you'd discovered that the fall from eternity,
here, in the spinout from cloudburst to ground,

is nothing compared to the sudden shock and glue
of gravity, sealing you here onto this tombstone:

I want to offer you this small sliver of orange—
I want to watch your bewildered thirsty mouth
close on the sliced tart and tang of a summer day
as mine, too, has learned to close itself on joy
and wonder, on this lemon, lime and tangerine,
as mine has learned to savor and to swallow
all these falling days imbued with hue and flavor.

I want to sit beneath you, here in your company,

as the songs of warblers, singing in the swamp rose
that's growing above this mushroom-stained lake,
orchestrate the sun's yellowed, buttery descent;

as the field daisies and bell flowers, climbing up
around your small, oyster-stained feet, tickle you

and enchant you into the hypnotic allure of sensation,
to this fervent hallucination of sound and sense,

as this sprawling oak tree, towering above you
like a dutiful guard, keeps its sturdy vigil on you.

How bright it must be for your exalted opened eyes—

as you witness the sunset dancing over the graves,
as you see the last birds flashing and soaring
through the pine trees in flight, as you discover
the wandering mourners leaving by the steel gate—

how frightening, how exhilarating, to be born awake.

Rose Mallow (Representation)

We are mirrors, says the rose mallow,
peeking up and lying still and languid

on the water's vitreous surface
as I kneel to her, my camera in hand.

Her pallid white face, powdered,
softly streaked in chalk, in talc.

Her crimson lips, puckered in the center
like an Asian choral dancer—

blowing me a sensual, nameless kiss.
Her delicate hands resting on water,

her thin streak of a body submerged,
hidden, so that when I reach for her

she drifts away, and the birds above us,
rouse up, fly into the colors of a storm.

Think of every lover you have kissed,
every supple body beneath your hand.

Is love the calling of the hidden organs—
bidding us to rise up for the first time

to test the harmony of our reach?
We are a formless circumstance—

testing what it feels like to matter.
Look, she says, at the Japanese beetles

that consume my face, at the frogs
and snakes that use my body for cover,

at the hummingbirds and bees that
offer their sweet pollen to my open lips.

We are representation, she says to me,
and we're just reflections for one another:

we're the sum of all our borrowings.

Vincent's Song

Tormented by the violent
slashes of swelling black crows

flying, erratic, over the corn,
and by the electric scintilla

of yellow light rising as stars
over the river Rhône,

and by the shades of azure blue
capturing the white chalky glaze

of the sky as it spreads west
and east over the vanishing city,

and, seized by the blunt tombstones
where the derelict orphans

duck in refuge under pine trees
the amazed hue of green liquor,

you surrendered to color—
to all of its hallucinogenic ways—

and you split yourself open, too,
at the edge of your chest

where your inner heart opened
up an eye, gleaming and radiant

and wide awake, and you weaved
and twisted yourself tightly

into an ambulant paintbrush,
an emergency, of art.

Sharon

By the dazed cubic light of the dusk's
wrinkling leaves and its tensing—

as the birds sang in the maple trees
and the stars rose, in white fencing,

and the mid-summer slugs opened up
and then constricted their wet bodies

like supple gel in the roaming roots
of the daisies and the tall coreopsis—

you kissed me gently on the lips,
Irish girl with the winsome eyes

and a mouth made of sweet mint.
This was long ago—before you were

married and a mother, and the years
of clouds and long streaming kites

roved and roamed the ginger skies
and the darkling beetles ate the wood—

and your body, soft, became abundant,
like a mayfly's darkened wing light

as it rose in caudal ferment over water;
and when the carnival's roasted heat

and the music turned loud, and the sky
became mandarin orange at sunset—

all those years ago when I remember
the telltale signs of your smile the best—

you and I fell back—against a church
wall—two dusky wing moths, to kiss.

Ashes

Who doesn't love the gray carbon
light of dusk,

the afterglow of the sun's fire,
descending in the roses?

The night's insect noises, made
of squeals and tears,

of the daylong mania of excited
light—

softening the surface of trees,
of roadsides, of buildings,

of people's cheeks as they stop,
visit with one another,

and kiss the sensual dayglow
between them, this romance of light.

Then, this carbon, ash-filled
descent,

this dénouement of daylong
self-control:

how it fills us with uncertainty,
with wanderlust, with roaming.

Once—at a campsite—in the hills,
and in the burning logs, as the moon

rose above the rhododendron
and it spilled its yellow butterflies

into the valley,
I saw in the emerging ashes

every lost and wasted year.
Saw how I would lose myself

inside my secrecy, my bark,
in my refusal to allow the embers

of a new threshold to beckon me—
and I saw how I would fail,

and still later be burned in a fire,
my body, caked in ashes,

in the evangelism of the flame's
holy christening—

in its ashen ritual of acceptance
and its worship of darkness into light,

my throat, marked by the wood's
blackened charcoal, its death mask—

my arms and hands stiffened out,
racooned in gray and chalk

(some upright spirit-ghost would I be:
all my becoming, born of this)

as I stretched up, felt the night
cloaking me in its transcendence

and blessing me back home—
to my ferocity, to my roaming—

in the moon's long, slow romance
with descent and ash,

and I felt the inexorable sliver
of my emigrant spirit

rising into flame, up in the embers
of carbon and soot

and holding fast to the idea
that, on every dark slope,

my inner light must always be
remembered:

and it said to me: *don't stop me—*
I'm just being born.

Amelie's Song

—for Anita

When the birds invaded the wild parsnip
   and rot carved black smudges
      like a cancer in the Queen Anne's lace,

and when the dame's rocket and yellow iris
   were flooded by a sudden storm squall
      that flatted them down like royal princesses

in ruined dresses, she wandered down
   into the lonesome motherwort
      to gather the whorls of white flowers

into her broken little arms for the funeral.
   And when the sweet clover and garlic mustard
      grew heavenward in the dry sun,

she knelt there at the edge of the pond,
   waiting for a bird she had heard
      calling out to the wind to come back down again

to her, so she could hear it sing. And when night fell,
   when she knew her mother would never
      return—because death had flooded her

just like bad blood floods the eyes of an animal
   just before it crawls off and it dies—
      she wandered to the open edge of the bog

where the nodding ladies' tresses grew wild there,
   in their décor of white flowers spiraling up thin
      adolescent bodies getting ready for their

autumn dancing, and then she laced them—
   one-by-one—to the sides of her head,
      where she flowered them there in her braids

for the next joyful dancing—and for all the dances
   that followed, all the years after that.
      And, at her wedding, she wore a pink

lady's slipper, and trails of purple-fringed orchids
   fell behind her wedding gown as she
      strode down the aisle there, into the sun.

Sermon of the Most Desiring

From the sliced fruit of morning sunlight
    smeared like a zesty
        market lemon
            over the river's

insistent tidal water;
    and from over the winter-beaten
        roads leading upward
            into the farmer's market

where jazz and blues triumphed
    over snow
        and over the frost's
            hoary gray beards

hanging in frozen icicles
    from the gutters
        and the rail posts
            of the market;

and from the tableau of cherry trees
    and peach trees
        in their first bloom,
            and from the songbirds'

most holy jubilee;
    and also from that quiet lot
        of forsaken and rusted
            Packards
                where you

fell to your knees
    one day
        in order to praise
            the chickadees

in their prayers of contrition—inside shrubs
    dense with berries
        and with
            religious fervor—

and from the transmigrated people,
          come here to shop
                    for fresh meat
                              and for farm eggs

and asparagus and onions,
          and for wooden market crates
                    flooded with tropical fruit
                              and fresh green produce

and reams of tomatoes,
          carrots and berries,
                    leeks, yams, cauliflower,
                              lemons and lime—

comes the sermon of most desiring.
          All morning
                    you could hear it,
                              asking you,

"Tell me, how did you feel
          when you
                    came out of
                              the wilderness?"

"How did it feel to you
          to feel again
                    so free—
                              deep within your heart?"

All morning, in the excited yelps
          of sea gulls;
                    all morning,
                              in the faces

of the happy people
          whose hands held
                    and traded
                              fresh spice,

whose dogs panted gently,
          sniffing the air;
                    all morning,
                              as the street

drummers beat the tin cans
    and the bongos with young,
        energetic hands,
           and the trumpet player

blew his cold horn
    against a sky whose clouds
        threatened spring rain
          but instead

opened up into bright blue—
    a blue so vast the sky's
        broad palette could
          barely contain it—

you heard it
    deep in your most holy heart,
        the sermon
          of most desiring.

V

My Father's Song

Some men are born
gathering a nest

of white and dark,
fabulous musical notes

to them,
and some men,

born broken like two halves
of the April moon,

discover that to drink
alone at night—

under the glass chandelier's
metropolis of stars

shining over a boardwalk
where tugboats

usher in ships
whose melodic horns

blow mournful
refrains

over the bay's glow—
is to discover

the very edge
where heartache

and music, those twin
companions, prevail.

And so, at night,
they lift up

their strong arms,
and they carry their horns

under a twilight,
and they saunter out

where the moonlight glows
like a great partridge pea

hanging loose in the sky
so that they can feel

all that aloneness
there, holding court.

And then they blow their horns
to the moon,

and to the Goddess body,
and to the many bodies,

and to beauty
and to soul,

and to the vast category
of inscrutable love—

and thus is their benediction
many forms: a tuneful ladder.

And when they find it—
their song—

they become forsaken
by every sweet summer

night,
every lost love

they could never
hold tight,

and, within themselves,
smoked holy

with the music one feels
when one is blessed full

with camphor and blues,
they depart.

Kelly's Song

Little boy, whose blond hair
hangs like eastern hemlock

in your eyes as you bend
low to the soft, summer earth

to cup your gerbil in hand—
before it roams so quickly

out of sight beneath the mock
orange (where, years ago,

as the crickets chirruped, we saw
the feral cat skulking low,

waiting to pounce on something
unsuspecting)—I *see* you in my memory

in your hospital skullcap,
the sweating glass of ice water

lonesome for your lips
parched with thirst, as the December

snow light, pale as prairie warbler yellow,
falls dustily through the window

and settles in a circle on the floor.
When we ran together, before you

fell sick, you roamed behind me,
always inside some dream of life—

some form of reverie that seemed
part song sparrow, part fallen angel—

and you strayed, yards behind me,
as the autumn leaves fell,

like harvest butterflies, to the ground.
And when I stopped for you,

you huffed out that you were
sorry, and that you could not keep up,

your heart itself, being wounded
at birth like a punctured choke cherry;

and when you caught up to me,
puffing, you took my arm and pulled me

downward, toward the meadow, where
we rolled together, gasping, laughing,

and a dog rushed out at us, tail wagging,
its life one long nosing into adventure;

and when we started up again, running,
you rushed ahead of me, risking it,

your left arm raised taut in triumph,
and I let you roam ahead, in victory,

even though the world behind us—
the park and the surrounding streets,

collaged by trees, changing their hue—
flared so much in opalescent color,

and in so much vaporous beauty,
that we both stopped to stare back

into it, into the mirrored glass of this
one school day, glazed by autumn's

flawless light; and we were dumbstruck
by the sheen and gleam of it, this one

triumphant world rising jubilant
into manic color—into lithol red,

cobalt yellow, monarch orange—before
the stamina of its final stand fell prey

(*although your face, a boundless blaze, rose up
away*) to winter's heartsick gray.

Basswood Meditation

Creamy chartreuse puffy flowers hanging under tiny,
almost hidden wings—

hanging so delicate from the rafters
of the basswood tree leaves—

like the flowers are the afterwards tokens
of angels that have ceased to fly

or to even exist. Are long ago dead. *I see you.*

The opening is always inside the light.
And so it is—after you have been stilled

and quieted, and mournful,
and deep into yourself,

way out here in the breezy meadow
where the chattering call notes

of the chickadees, hidden in the old basswood tree

that's about to fall over, roust you out of your
silence—

so it is again that you find your eyes are alerted,
yet again,

to just this world: so soft, so excited into frenzy
by the sunlight, by this scintillant shining,

passing over the osier dogwood

and through the dark, dry shadows
of the melancholy woods,

and into the tangles of nameless shrubs
where the dirt, under them,

is also a graveyard to some.

And, as you hold in your hand the photograph
of the little blond boy

whose death occurred so very long ago,

you feel again that endless light inside of you,
that light that never tires

of its awakening in you again, to go on
one more day, carrying it, inside of you,

this little light that is the light of all those who've
lived inside you—

your one little flame-bearing torch; your liberty light.

It's as if, within all memory, there is a string of fragrant chartreuse
flowers

hanging from thin wing-like structures, ceiling rafters.

It's as if memory, like love, carries always within it
youth—

that one unconquerable whorl of excitable light
that shows us who we are: how we must go on, unvanquished.

When someone dies, their light becomes in you
your light,

if you will it so. *Every life a light,* a fragrant chartreuse flower,
an ignited sunbeam.

And, through the opening slots of the heart-shaped tree leaves
cut with light—

and, within the sound-cloud of a buzzing cacophony
you can't quite comprehend

with your intellect's sharp, dismissive edge—
you see the hordes of bees gathering,

like a multitude, like a splendid momentum
here above you,

where the sky's bright opening, the day's deep portal,

lets all the other vivid lights of what you deeply love
in.

What the Tomatoes Say to Me

All along the green waterfall,
the red hearts fall and abide,

and some gleam and shine,
polished by the afternoon's pride,

while others, those down
near the earth's sullen wetness,

are torn open, are ravished
by fruit worms and birds

and by stink bugs climbing in
to burrow their holes.

And, when startled, I kneel
to find some tomatoes

discolored in blossom-end rot,
some cat-faced and gruesome,

some zippered and scarred,
as if in the after-cut of surgery,

and some, those nearest to dirt,
crackling and bursting open

in disease, or in some other
kind of afternoon rapture,

or I find some, spotted
with yellow halos, while others—

those marauded and violated
by birds and spilled open, wet,

and scabbed over with crusts,
with sun-scalded, old-age blight—

fall hapless, like old widows,
into the faded mat of dirt

while still others, those upright,
seem to rise heavenward, to light.

Scavenger's Lullaby

Marsh marigold and woundwort,
heal-all and spotted jewelweed:

the marsh's collected works on display.
And a common yellowthroat warbler—

the male's bandit mask shrouded
in black, set off by its yellow throat—

skulking low in the boneset,
hunting for small insects and spiders.

You can hear its *chuck, chuck* and its
cheeping, *witchity-whichity,* as the frogs

burp out in refrain, and the toads,
heavy-hearted, blurt and they bellow.

These tiny fragments of memory!
Potpourri of your heart's floral cup:

look at all the faces and places we visit
just to gather a cupful of souvenirs.

The catch-all of the memorable pictures
in your mind's rounded frame.

Aren't we scavengers, you think—
just moving bandits, wing-jumping

through life's momentary thickets?
Now her face, rising to greet you

on your wedding night; now gone
so quickly, we gather in the red dust.

Now you scavenge again, find her,
standing at the edge of the marsh:

your eyes—alert like a bandit's—
rummaging through the last light.

Forgiveness Lullaby

Freedom is the possibility of being generous
—*Chogyam Trungpa*

Under the bridge's rumble and laughter,
the yellow daisies' uproar and refrain,

the cicada's improvisational line of buzzing
and the river's slow unveiling of suspension—

as the wind's spirited mood, and its breezes,
invades and inebriates all the buzzing bees—

you hear, in the blue afterglow of the day's
slow and steady abandonment of sound,

your *forgiveness lullaby,* so gentle and so true,
sounding up like a gentle strum of chords.

I think it must come from a songbird's manic
recitation of the sky's changing of its colors;

all this gilded copper light and this music:
this perpetual shifting of tone and melody

casting pigmentation over the river's rippling
of moss and shadow, these fauves and greens.

I think I hear my soft lament, my evening's
refrain—my forgiveness lullaby—so dense

with silence and with all those words I did
or did not say to those I've loved or lost

in the evening's quick, revealing garden.
And in the bruised mossy shading, beneath

the bridge's vaulted curve and its trenchant echo,
I hear this lullaby, calming my hurt again

and softening me—no matter the hour's
delay—and it feels to me so very complete,

so very true: this reconciliation lullaby
passing the bitter fracture of regret away.

Isn't it so very true, that mourning enters
one into a different, slower threshold of time?

And, within this mourning time, memories
pass not above or below, but through one

another—like blotches changing into liberated
colors, or like notes floating through a violin—

and by so doing, by being within this mourning
time, hurt, and the solidified facts of it,

changes for us; we roam outside the tight grip
of history, and we release ourselves, we forgive.

All the words, said or unsaid, to the other at last
are offered up, are released without harm to anyone.

I think it must be the way the heart is calmed
when the mind, obliterated by time, *silences*;

and it is filtered—this burdened mind—by the
strength of a mourning moving through it.

And so you kneel there, holding a picture
in your hands, listening to your forgiveness—

as the hours of this one day slip and fall
into a wandering coda, like an afternote—

and you listen, *within,* to where the old injury
becomes mended and sewn into a new zipper,

this resolving speech that's so short in you;
so kind and so thick with the heart's soft

generosity; its freedom reconciliation—where
you're released from torment, from memory's

traumatic interweave of hurt and deep regret.
And you hear it—so softly—rising up in you,

this forgiveness lullaby, releasing you—
from all this night-born guilt and harm.

Medicine Circle

All night the stars in the sky exploded like rattles,
    and they fell to the earth

like granite fragments into the medicine circle
    that I'd chosen for myself;

and, once, struck by one of those bright stones,
    I no longer felt so afraid of the frigid icing

of the stars and the floating moon
    swirling above me in electrified loneliness.

A small frog jumped into my circle.
    I watched it long-jump a pile of oak leaves,

and it landed right next to my quivering hand
    as I held a flashlight to it,

and then it hopped into my open palm
    and I felt it mark me—quickly—

across the long vein there like an inoculation
    against something I'd always dreaded,

which then became the clan I would belong to—
    amphibious, croaking, poetic.

And I knew the shape of my solid bones
    into liquids, and the red blood

coursing through my wrist
    became a wiggling snake as I lifted

a dewy rock to hold it high
    to the moon ascending wide awake—

and, suddenly, I entered the galaxy in a canoe,
    and I rowed the universe alone.

And the night insects rose and fell
    around me

in an electric, translucent bourrée,
    in a kind of silent delirium,

until I became quenched of all the thirst
    that my intellectual reason

had choked to dry dirt inside of me.
    And, sometime, during the final act

of my night-rowing dream, I was baptized
    in a raging thunderstorm—

which then became my new medicine name
    against all the other names

that had misidentified me for years upon years
    as just this man of preoccupation and skin.

On the west coast of Michigan, in Petoskey,
    my father—after fishing—

collapsed into the silent, foam-filled truncation
    of a heart attack, and he

slowly slipped through an opened portal
    like a silenced guitar,

his skeleton, like a Les Paul guitar box,
    shattered asunder,

the silver strings of his rib cage
    snapping open to release his soul.

I felt the pulsing of death roaming through me,
    and I broke open like a star.

And, from then onward, I felt death
    walking deep within me like traveler

wearing my name and then again *no name*
    at all, except for expansion and vibration.

Something cemented and bolted in me
    was split open—like a sudden splay

of scattered bones and metals—
    and the forces at work in me

became an enlivened momentum of roots
    spreading not downward

but *outward,* like roaming rings or like sleek contours
    of shattered water and luminescence

spreading the rest of me beyond me—
    like filaments of traveling light.

And then I rolled over and slept. I felt
    the imperceptible, the clandestine,

the unexplored, and the world of my future
    like an expanding pulse of emanation.

And I was told to begin the full erasing
    of my personhood

and the reconstitution of my selfhood
    as a ribbon of running water that sings.

At four a.m., I heard the urgent calls of a shriek owl
    piercing my dream in the pines.

At dawn, the sun melted
    through the opaque range

of morning clouds spreading across
    the horizon,

and a new man strolled
    through the swamp sumac

as if he were a mysterious messenger
    blessing me home.

Grief Again (The Goddess Tells Me How to Purify)

She *said,* pour your thoughts over hot stones.
Go ahead and pour all this grief and sadness
over you; do you really think we gain
anything by running from it?
So curl your wounded selfhood under it,
this wetness, this rage and anger;
this obtuse and blinding melancholy in you;
and let your whole neck and shoulders drown in it
until you are nothing more than darkened rags
beneath it. Only then will you feel
the undesirable in you become a quality
of nothing, just mineral water rinsing over
a ledge of hot stones within you.
And this secret craving of loss that incites you:
do you really believe you can remain immune
from it? And she *said,* pour your thoughts over
these hot stones. You're only water, in and through
your body's lodge; your long-lasting life episode
merely a blueprint, a *contour*—of patterns
and placements, of emotional gestures.
You have entered here to wash away all residue
of what you've held on to or lost to heartache.
Your life, one long reconstitution of itself:
Love itself, and life and death, this changing circumstance.
This riverbed where the streams of livingness move
through you. You must give all this injury away,
all this hurt within you; all this astonished certainty
in yourself that blocks you from the *shock point*
of loss—you see, your bulwark is only make-believe.
And you're just a sky lantern composed of thin
rice-paper sheets; your soul, an aura, deep inside you.
And it holds a candle that burns eternally for you;
it burns like this, every day for you,
and you are lifted up in it—as the whole lantern
is uplifted by the flame and winds that stir it—
This, she said, is how you will come to *revelation*;
and, she said, you must *see* the intangible in you:
for you still insist that you can possess it
through a *simple clinging to it*; and this procession
of images that your grief provides to you—

at dawn, at the hour of sleep, when you long
for the return to what was once named by love,
or by unity, or by certainty—*is gone.* For there can be
no return to the old intimacies you hold so dear,
for they, too, are just the fleeting immediacies
of time's passing. And in the long silences
you feel in here—in this wet darkness—
please know that you're just a host of relationships,
just a cartography of all this deep happenstance
and imagination; and please know that you love,
and are loved, just as much in ignorance
as you are loved in charity—this is always
the nature of the beloved and the beholden—
and so you must rise up, in this mutiny and delight,
or else you'll remain inside doubt and sadness
all your days. I can't tell it to you any better
than this: your thoughts, ideas, *just insubstantial bulk.*
Just pour your thoughts over these hot stones.
Pour the cup of flawless water over
what's frozen up in you—and, then, stream
and flow it freely across these red-hot stones
so that the steam arises wet and angry.
Feel this wrath and fury overtake you,
this deep displeasure; and, then, loft the water
over your weary head, spill it over where your heart
and mind burn hottest; where disconsolation
hardens you toward woe; and, then, wash it over outrage,
fits and temper, over this despondency and this
despair; and let yourself be awake to what forms
of relief are rinsed out in you; and, now, allow this
transformed sadness—all this woe and sorrow—
to *dissipate* in you; let it rinse you out, let it
purify you as you enter into your healing's
woven clove. Only then will you know solace.
This epiphany you hold through your surrender.
This innocence in you that makes you live again.
All the rest of it—this failure to circulate
your grief and your rapture, all this cloudburst
of desire in you that reaches upward into
loneliness, into holiness, into ecstatic treasure?

Well, leave it alone for now: it's only a
quality of deep grace and fullness—*both*—
and nothing of it stays too long in your possession.
Your life's *pine cone*—like a whirling dervish—
is one long flawless unshaping of its seed
into ether; you're just one long translation—
into this nameless mineral and light.

Recitation of the Wind on a Country Road

Surrounding the rising little butterfly
    that you see—flying out from the purple
fringed orchid like a small white Chinese lantern

up into the afternoon's bronzed coloration—
    is a kind of *particle light*.

Inside this particle light—these infinite and durable
    intensities and variations of light—

is a measure of time-light, and the everlasting life
    of an event.

And inside all that are the elements of creation
    that make up a life.

You watch it, this event of dust-particulate
    and fascinated halo-light,

as this one butterfly, perfect in itself, spreads
its wings inside the wind's billowing scarf,

and it, too, becomes a style of flight.
    Last week, at the art opening, where

large rectangles and obelisks were shown
    as measurements of time, I didn't believe

in wind, in swarms, in a set of speeds
    by which everything I *was* worked.

It seemed all reality was a measurement
    of geometry, of quantity.

All these shapes, constructed, displayed,
became a kind of prankish, aesthetic revelation.

Now, though, it is different: I am the effect
    of all my events. This is so.

And all my events are the effect of me.

And so I watch the light join the wind
    and become the pattern of a snake

as it catches a clump of bluestem grass
        and cut weeds, and the wind tosses it

so that it whips up, spirals, flattens like flung
        seed and drops, listless, to the road.

Now this snake-in-the-wind is shapeless,
        its assemblage unpredictable, potent.

The storm, gathering up above me, turns
        the horizon moonstone gray.

I don't know where the road stops, where wind roars the sea.
Alongside me, the vast meadow bends and rises.

Behind me, tall pine trees wave
        where the wind—an infinity of meetings and partings—

slices through the immediacy where
        I walk. And as I feel it,

I think, *I am the wind*. I am the listless, infinite direction.
I am this longitude and this latitude that the wind speaks of:

If the wind says it's so, I must be—no more, no less—

just a multiplicity of smaller and larger possibilities.

I am a riddle of composition: a movement, a rest,
        a speed and a slowness. A changeableness.

Some of me moving fast enough to keep up,
        some of me, not.

Death is not a mistake:
It is a line of filament we ramble over.

The self must be a multiplicity threshold.

        I am the wind.

Poem for the Dying in Ascent

Rising up from the lush green
hosta leaves, the small

ascent goddess—masquerading
as a perfumed fragrance

atop the delicate white flowers—
whispers of the ascent:

how it is we swirl up from the body
threads of our cocoon of skin,

leaving our muscles behind,
our bones made of yellow turnips;

our blood vessels and arteries
assembled from pomegranate

and ambrosia marinade;
our cells, our dendrites, our wiry axons

separating themselves from
pride and shame, from humiliation,

and from all other lost
passions: the touch of fingers,

the kiss on the lips, on eyelids
composed of exquisite firelight;

and we ascend, we soar like particles
breaking into filaments of glint,

or perhaps as a comet in rising ascent
to meet just our selves

at the uppermost rim
where the treetops

radiate the sunset's dazzled glare;
as the universe's sharp claw

slices the whole moon in half
in a split flare as it floats

through the dark sky to commemorate
its long sojourn

through the starless infinitude.
You are *here,* she says—

oh small irrelevance of mercy,
oh tiny speck of reason's

insufferable glow; oh excited
whirl and dervish

of this cycle of time.
Rise, now, as wind and music;

as a single line of stars
climbing a vine;

as a choiceless awareness—
ignited in propulsion and flight.

Rise in the eternal light
of melody and threnody

until, at the edge of the sky,
you see below you

a column of dust,
a decanter, emptying—

and rise up, *spirit,*
to your secret impulse.

Wisdom Deity

After the raining, the storms, in the swell
of the morning after—

and amidst the ungathered melee
of dinner plates and wine glasses

and browned coffee cups and funeral flowers
sprawled all over the kitchen counter,
the summer deck—

the small wisdom deity, that swift-moving blink of an eye,
entered the immeasurable light and manifested

on the face of a fragrant Eros lily.

She announced she knew *absolutely nothing*.

Suggested we contemplate it, this nothingness
that now scrambled through the ferns,

took shape as a chipmunk withdrawing into a burrow
to perish in a firmament of moss and moisture.

Look at the judgment of fire and minerals, she said,

so that this aeon of marriage—this rogue Sophia deity
of matter and ether—can again and again

be contemplated,
she said. We who are—and are nowhere, standing.

We are the ones who have come to live
in this unchangeable aeon. This, our world, she said.

Body, flesh, matter, purity, and gaseous afterthought.

The thoroughfares of our holy garments: body and spirit.

Oh, and of *mourning,* she said: this ongoing collection
of the ungathered and ungatherable particulars.

This careful memory, what mourning truly is—
the iniquity, made whole.

But not in pursuit of a security object. There is no such entity,
she said. More like a dissipating cloud. Yes.

You are here to gather them all—these points
of immeasurable light—into your seized
garments. Your belly. Your body.

Into the folds of your stiff earth, your
dissipating shield, your time lapse of indwelling.

They are for the ungathering of your final days.
Oh flying dust. Oh fleeting dream.

Vesper Sermon for the Night Songs

Oh you speakeasy roustabout
songs of the ducks on the river;

you kickbacks of logs, falling over,
and treetop branches, capsizing

into the hurl and glow of the water
bubbling outward, down and over;

you ruckus of squirrels chasing
each other through collapsed hickory

trees and the fallen stone cathedrals
of the river's economy of gray turning;

oh you last known songs of birds
echoing through dew and red bramble;

you high lonesome calls of the owl,
hooting it up to the rising white moon;

you invisible reed and sedge warblers
singing to the night's gray etching;

you low-sprawling whippoorwills
with your three-syllable calls, eating

your fill of beetles and mosquitoes
and all the other night-flying bugs;

oh you long-drawn-out dry language
of tree branches snarled by wind

and by the loose, silk dragging skirts
of the river as it dredges itself home;

you root-snarled mud shrubs, tangled
up with kites and other plastic fiber;

oh you ignoble, hanging decorations
of tennis shoes and looping hoodies

draped over the cartography of trees;
oh you decorative emblems of refuse

tossed into the river's wet orphanage
from hikers who've strayed behind;

you nasal songs of nighthawks booming
over me as I wander down through it all;

oh you incessant burping of toads—
murmuring and belching by night;

you one-after-another cricket songs
and somnambulant slur and ember

of insect actions filling the dark radius
of the river's lower walk with singing;

oh you insufferable katydids rubbing
your self-names, your lisps and tics

into hot wings of starlight and magic
through the tattered scarlet foliage

bent to dereliction and root rot—
into this impregnable night's glowing;

oh you last-known songs of dusk—
melodies mysterious and evanescent,

melodies only the night walker
can know when walking through here

with all the bones of himself drunk
and dazed by the milk of the moon—

Come into me and engage me.
Make me one with your drone.

Acknowledgments

Algebra of Owls: "Amelie's Song"
Bryant Literary Review: "Aspects of Kelly's Death"
Burningwood Literary Journal: "My Father's Song"
Collateral Damage Anthology: "Dwayne's Song (Child of the Moon)"
Common Ground Review: "Ropes"
Dressing Room Poetry Journal: "The Song of the Letting It All Go"
Firefly: "Song for the Dying as a Song," "Invocation," "What the
    Tomatoes Say to Me"
Freshwater: "Statue"
Gravel Magazine: "Song for DS"
Kentucky Review: "These Days"
Lullwater Review: "Mourning Song"
Muddy River Poetry Review: "Sermon of the Mourning Dove"
Origins Journal: "December 9th 1980," "Limelight"
Panopoly: "Grief"
Peninsula Poets: "Mortal Lullabies," "Uncle Joe's Song"
Pirene's Fountain: "Medicine Circle," "Watching Bilal Fall,"
    "Rose Mallow (Representation)"
Public Pool: "Ashes"
Rattle: "Car Accident"
Skylight 47: "Poem for a Homeless Woman"
The Bookends Review: "Vincent's Song"
The Broken Plate: "Chopin's Prelude Op. 28 No. 15"
Third Wednesday: "The Small Sculpture Angel," "MD"

"Car Accident" was an honorable mention selection in the 2006
Rattle Poetry Prize competition.

"Watching Bilal Fall" is the winner of the 2015 *Pirene's Fountain*
Liakoura Prize.

About FutureCycle Press

FutureCycle Press is dedicated to publishing worthwhile English-language poetry books, chapbooks, and anthologies in both print-on-demand (POD) and Kindle ebook formats. Founded in 2007 by long-time independent editor/publishers and partners Diane Kistner and Robert S. King, the press incorporated as a nonprofit in 2012. A number of our editors are distinguished poets and writers in their own right, and we have been actively involved in the small press movement going back to the early seventies.

The FutureCycle Poetry Book Prize and honorarium is awarded annually for the best full-length volume of poetry we publish in a calendar year. Introduced in 2013, our Good Works projects are anthologies devoted to issues of universal significance, with all proceeds donated to a related worthy cause. Our Selected Poems series highlights contemporary poets with a substantial body of work to their credit; with this series we strive to resurrect work that has had limited distribution and is now out of print.

We are dedicated to giving all of the authors we publish the care their work deserves, making our catalog of titles the most diverse and distinguished it can be, and paying forward any earnings to fund more great books.

We've learned a few things about independent publishing over the years. We've also evolved a unique, resilient publishing model that allows us to focus mainly on vetting and preserving for posterity poetry collections of exceptional quality without becoming overwhelmed with bookkeeping and mailing, fundraising activities, or taxing editorial and production "bubbles." To find out more about what we are doing, come see us at www.futurecycle.org.